FAIL SAFE
PLANNING

BECAUSE FAILING TO PLAN IS PLANNING TO FAIL.

To Sarah,
This is for you and
to your success!
best,
Rick

TABLE OF CONTENTS

PREFACE

The old adage is, "failing to plan in a business is the same as planning to fail".

For those of you who routinely struggle in your business and repeatedly fail to plan, this book is for you.

This book is for you because I can show you how easy it is to create successful plans for your organization. It has been consistently proven that having and executing a plan will lead you to greater success.

Through working with many businesses as a Business/Executive Coach, I can substantiate the fact that most fail to plan. I predominantly work with privately held small and medium-sized businesses and can confirm that in this market space, over 98% do not do any business planning.

I further believe that the reason there is a lack of planning is for two reasons:

- They simply do not know how to plan.

  In this book, I will show you a very easy, very effective way to create a plan for your business. This is **not** a plan to start a business. I will show you the way to create an ongoing, strategic business plan. (I know...strategic is a very scary word, isn't it!?)

- They do not believe in the positive benefits of planning.

In over 12 years of helping clients reach new heights, I can give countless great examples of how planning has transformed businesses, and how strategic plans have led companies to amazing successes.

The US SBA, as well as many consulting organizations, have even conducted studies on the effectiveness of business planning and all have come to the same conclusion. Business planning leads to greater success!

Still not convinced? Google it and read the results for yourself!

Come along with me as we go through a quick journey on a very successful, simplistic way to start business planning. If after reading this you're still not convinced, visit our website, or call us:

Rick Munson
Business/Executive Coach
Paramount Business Development, Inc.
www.paramountbusinessdevelopment.com
745 Main Street
Suite 205
Stroudsburg, PA 18360
1-570-517-7100

ACKNOWLEDGEMENTS

This may be hard to understand as you are reading this…. But I hate to write. I do everything possible to not have to write. I am slow at it, I am lousy at it…oh, and did I mention I hate it!?

So as you are reading this, I must thank those that really made this possible.

Jenny Kane. The most amazing Administrative/Marketing Assistant. Through her thorough and quiet ways, she kept encouraging me to do this. She has been extremely supportive in this effort, and most importantly in our business in general.

Bill Skinner. One of the nicest people I know and the best business partner that I could ever ask for. Bill wrote a book last year, "Sales Magic: 12 Steps to Achieve Massive Sales Growth," at our urging. What a great book! So now the pressure has been on me!

Andrew Neitlich. Andrew is the best coach I know. He is a great colleague and mentor. He is the CEO and the driving force behind The Center for Executive Coaching. He has consistently urged me to write this book, citing that the business market "needs it."

Paramount Business Development clients. You all know who you are and almost all of you have been through this process at least once, if not many times. While you do not realize it, you are all my inspiration. Everything I do is for you! You are what motivates me and keeps me going! Thank you!

Cheryl Henderschedt. Cheryl, my wife, my love, my daily inspiration! You are always a steadfast believer and a constant steady supporter. Without you, many things would not be possible. Thank you for always being there!

THE BROTHERS SHIM RUN OUT OF GAS

Three brothers, Tom, Dick, and Harry, always dreamed of being business owners while growing up. Their father, Jack, was a small business owner and they all looked up to him and respected his perks as a business owner: handsome rewards, flexibility, autonomy, the whole thing.

As Tom, Dick, and Harry grew up and graduated high school, they started going their own ways. Each following their specific interests, but steadfastly holding to their ideals of being business owners.

Tom graduated high school and due to his love of cars, immediately became an auto mechanic. At first he worked for dealership repair shops, but eventually he gravitated to high-end private repair shops. Ultimately, after working for others for about 20 years, he had an opportunity to buy a neighboring shop from a retiring owner. Due to his status and respect in the community, he was able to get a very good deal on the purchase.

By this time, Tom had built quite a reputation and a following as "the fix it guy." Tom had immediate customers and modest success upon buying his own garage. Tom was a pro mechanic.

Dick was always fascinated with building things as a child. He built structures from Lincoln Logs, then Legos, and eventually graduated up to building forts in the woods behind their childhood home. Upon graduating high school, Dick went to trade school to learn carpentry and masonry. Dick immediately found employment for a general contractor. He quickly moved up through the ranks to more and more responsibility and higher roles. Eventually, he became an estimator and ultimately company President, working directly for the owner.

Then the day came that there was a particularly contentious large project that was not going well and profitability was in serious doubt. This caused serious issues between Dick and the owner. The issues became unsurmountable in Dick's mind due to some values-based decisions that Dick could not come to terms with. Ultimately, Dick left and started his own general contracting business.

Dick was well known in the construction business and was a good leader. Most admired Dick because of his strong set of values and high integrity. It wasn't long before Dick's new general contracting business was doing well. He had a strong book of business, large projects, and was growing quickly.

Harry took a completely different path from his brothers. Harry was much more technical in his approach and took a fine interest in engineering. After high school, Harry enrolled in a prestigious school and soon earned a degree in mechanical engineering. Harry later went to work at a manufacturing company as a manufacturing engineer.

Harry had a penchant for efficiency and quality. He was highly focused on processes and how to make them more efficient and lower cost, while improving the quality of the output. Harry quickly brought acclaim to himself, not only within his company, but also within their specific industry.

Over time, Harry continued to advance in management. He went from maintenance engineering to project engineering to plant engineering, manufacturing manager, and ultimately ended up as general manager. During this whole time, he still wanted more. He wanted to own his own manufacturing company.

One day, that opportunity came. He was offered the opportunity to buy the company he was general manager for. He jumped at the chance.

By the time they had reached their mid-forties, all three of the brothers Shim; Tom, Dick, and Harry were all business owners. All was right in the world!

Until.

Well, until it wasn't.

The brothers remained close throughout life, physically and personally. However, their personal closeness usually revolved around family, kids, and their elderly parents. While not living in the same town, they all three lived in the same region.

They talked between themselves frequently on the phone, but rarely did the conversation turn to business topics. When it did, it was typically about a significant recent success. In-person meetings usually revolved around personal events such as birthdays and holidays. The families remained close over time.

Their most recent event was over the Thanksgiving holidays when they were all gathered at their parents' home. As was common after the family meal, the family would retire to the family room, or game room. All the kids were becoming teenagers and early adults and were very active.

On this particular holiday, the ladies and the children had all gathered in the family room to play games. Dick and Tom each grabbed a cup of coffee and headed out to the screened in porch to catch some fresh air and chat.

Not long after cleaning up, Harry walked out to the porch and found Tom and Dick in a deep discussion about business. Even though Harry was very interested in the topic, he was reluctant to interrupt or jump in.

Tom and Dick were both discussing their frustrations with their individual businesses and how while both were successful, they seemed stymied for growth and better returns. They were both apparently dealing with teams that were merely going through the motions in their opinions. Both were of the strong opinion that their respective teams were barely doing the minimum.

Tom and Dick's issues, while mostly similar, did have some critical differences.

Tom and his car repair business still seemed to be growing, although only slightly at this time. Tom was experiencing frustration because he was not reaching his growth targets and he still was not able to justify the expansion that he had hoped to do 2 years ago. Furthermore, he had been experiencing some customer satisfaction issues that in the past had been an extremely rare occurrence. It seemed like his team was simply not motivated as they had been when he was struggling to get established.

Dick, while having similar issues with his construction company, was mostly frustrated with his lack of being able to bring projects in on time and within budget. Another issue was that he was getting significant call backs to finish and/or to correct small issues. Dick's feeling was that his team had become somewhat apathetic and stopped paying attention to the small details. In the past, Dick's company had been known for flawless work and bringing projects in on time. Now, Dick's thoughts were surrounding the ever pickier and demanding customer base.

Harry listened to all the above with rapt attention. While his issues were different, he too was experiencing much frustration in today's world. Harry felt listless and numb to all the problems he was having. He vocalized that he was getting tired and just felt like a ship adrift without a rudder.

The brothers continued to commiserate for some considerable time, comparing notes and experiences. All admitted that they seemed stuck and without a plan, or knowledge of how to move forward.

While all three brothers were successful in their businesses, they all agreed that there was huge potential in their respective companies. They all agreed that they should be able to move forward to a higher level of growth and success but had no knowledge of how to do that.

As they sat and kept talking, the brothers all came to the same eureka moment! They needed to set new goals! They needed a plan! They needed a business plan! But how?

The brothers were all great problem solvers. They had each overcome significant hurdles in their lives by solving their way through. They set these skills in motion to solve this problem. They each were convinced that establishing a plan for their businesses would be the path to success. But not one of them had a clue on how to do it.

They all agreed to meet again within a few weeks, and meanwhile each of them would look for a way, and help, to start business planning…. (to be continued).

This is a common malady of businesses. All three of the brothers businesses got a bang of an initial start. Over time, after the initial period, complacency and a lack of focus and direction set in. This is quite common.

When businesses are young, recently bought, or just getting started, there is often a great deal of focus for mere survival and getting established. Over time, the initial objectives and goals get met, or given up on, and the original motivation and energy starts to fade. What eventually sets in is day-to-day "firefighting" or simply tending to the most urgent issues.

When asked, most business leaders in this mode simply report that they "do not have time" for business planning, or a higher level of thinking. Thus the process feeds on itself and the symptoms resulting from "firefighting" start to mushroom.

But it doesn't have to be that way! Businesses do not need to fail!

Business is easy. Business concepts are simple. Hard work! But simple and easy.

This book will show you how easy and straight-forward strategic business planning really is. Follow the steps. Whether you are a business leader, or a business service company, you will find this process very simple to follow.

The corporate world is rife with consultants that help them do strategic business planning. But alas, there is not much help for the private business owners. Most books and articles written about business planning are written at the Fortune 500 company level. This book is different. This book is written with the private company leader in mind.

So, don't get stuck. Don't procrastinate. Your future depends on it!

If you get stuck, or need help, call us. Today!

THE MORE THINGS CHANGE, THE MORE THEY STAY THE SAME

Not much has changed in the business world in over a hundred years, if not more. The same business principles still work today that worked then. A successful business is still about providing a product and/or service successfully to customers.

Some of my favorite books are "old" business books. One of my favorite authors is Napoleon Hill. His mindset principles that worked in the 1920s are still very valuable and work today.

So what has changed?

The people have changed! In the last 100 years, we have seen successive new generations; WWI Generation, WWII Generation, Silent Generation, Baby Boomers, Gen X, Millennials, and now Gen Z, or i Gen. Yes the people have changed, values have changed, preferences have changed, and likes/dislikes have changed. Yet, much remains the same.

Market needs have changed! Imagine the new things that we cannot live without. Televisions, cell phones, cars, and the list goes on.

The internet is new in business over the last 20 years and information is more readily, and more quickly, available than ever! But in the case of business planning, that does not mean we do it more, or more successfully!

Even with the advent of easily attainable information via the internet, it does not guarantee that the right things get done, or that things get done right!

A few months ago, I met a business owner that just might be the most well-read, up to date business owner I have met in a long while. However, he was very anxious to hire me as his Business Coach. At first, it was a bit puzzling.

After getting to know him, I soon began to understand why. His plight is the same as many and not uncommon in this information-rich world. He had a problem with knowing where and how to start. He further had a big problem with accountability, and moving himself forward!

For those of you that see yourself in him, this book is a step-by-step guide to making it happen. To keep yourself moving forward for the first time, bite off one chapter a week. And hold yourself to it!

Chapter 1: Establishing the Right Process

Paramount's Plan for Success Process
Strategic Planning Made Easy.

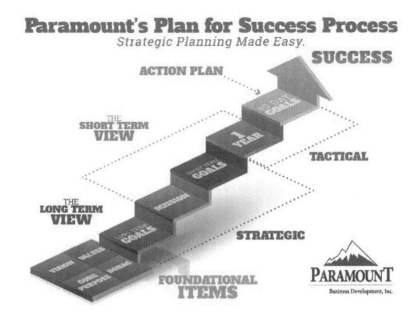

a. WHAT'S YOUR DESIRED DESTINATION?

I read a lot of business books. Correction: I start reading a lot of business books. With my experience in the last few years, I have learned to **stop** reading bad business books!

A couple of years ago, the Wall Street Journal reported that over 4,000 new business books had been published that previous year. I got to thinking, "I wonder how many of them were good business books?"

In my own study of my personal experiences, admittedly a very small sample size, less than 10% of the business books that I read contained new material that was worth the ink and the paper it was written on! My learning? Be careful what you read and what you believe in!

To that end, not long ago, I picked up a book on strategic business planning. There are undeniably very few available in print on this subject.

After reading the first 2 chapters, and perusing the table of contents, **I threw the book away!** Why? It had the process for planning all backwards!

The absolute best advice for beginning strategic business planning is to "begin with the end in mind." I believe this is a phrase coined by the late, great Stephen Covey in his bestselling book, "The 7 Habits of Highly Effective People."

This is the best way to begin business planning. How would you know where to start if you don't know where you want to end up?

I like to use parallels in my life and in my coaching. I compare business planning to taking a vacation. If I am going to go away on a vacation, I must know where I am going to go!

If I am going to vacation at Disney Land in Los Angeles, why would I want to start out by going to France first!?!?

So to put it in a better context, if I am going to grow my business, it is most efficient to know what my long range vision is for my business. Once I know that, I can make specific plans to make the path getting there very efficient.

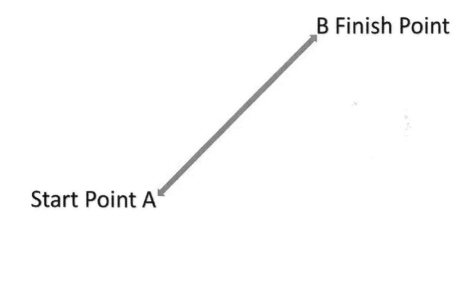

B Finish Point

Start Point A

b. SKIP THE SCENIC VIEW

As I am planning my vacation, it is most efficient to take the most direct routes available to get there, and limit the side trips as much as possible. The same is true with my business. That is why it is imperative to "start with the end in mind" and keep the side trips, I.e. diversions, distractions, etc., to a minimum.

Many businesses get distracted with things that are not relevant, and in many cases, relevant to anything! When you start with the end in mind, the thought is to keep everything congruent. If I am a car repair shop, why would I want to take a diversion into draperies? That is a pretty obvious example, yet, in my profession as a Business Coach, I see similar diversions frequently and dramatically.

Why do businesses do this? Is this a lack of focus? Is this bending to the whims of a spouse? An employee, a dream, or a glittery object in the distance? I do not know. What I do know is that it is very damaging to the business.

A successful business stays focused and is really good at one, or a very select few, things.

c. KNOW WHERE YOU DON'T WANT TO GO!

One way to stay relevant and not get off track is to set boundaries. What I mean is to be clear about what you do, and what you do not do. Unfortunately, many businesses get fearful that by establishing what they do not do will make them miss out on the "mother lode." However, it has been repeated by many that the most successful businesses are successful because they do one, or a few, thing(s) really well.

In my example of a car repair shop, it would be very hard for the owner of that business to be good at general car repairs, transmissions, tires, and body work. So, my wise car repair shop delineates very clearly that they do general car repairs on late model cars.

If you need transmission work, tires, or body work, he is very happy to refer you to trusted specialists in those areas. And if you have an old hot rod, or a classic car, all of which take specific knowledge and specific hard to find parts, he will recommend you to a specialist in that area as well.

Can you imagine trying to be good in all of those areas? It would be next to impossible.

So the concept of setting boundaries is to also know, very clearly, what you do not do.

d. THE STRATEGIC OUTLOOK

The concept of the strategic outlook is that a business owner does not work in a vacuum. What I mean is that the business owner needs to consider:

His local economy

His local market

His competitors

His longer range view of things

Such as: How is he going to stay relevant to his customers?

How is he going to continue to be the market's best choice?

The idea is to strategize how to continue to be successful and grow well in the future.

The unwise business owner only thinks about tomorrow and maybe next week.

In my example of the car repair shop owner, he needs to be looking at the general population in his market, the new car trends, the maintenance needs of the new cars, and his view of the competition, and so on.

e. THE DIFFERENCE BETWEEN STRATEGIC & TACTICAL

Unfortunately, there is a lot of confusion about the strategic part of a business plan and the tactical part of a business plan. Per "the Webster's dictionary:"

Definition of strategy: a careful plan or method (used to obtain a desired outcome).

Or in the business use of the term, "a careful plan used to obtain a desired outcome usually with the intention of growing a business or beating a competitor."

A strategy is usually carefully selected based on studying a market, a group of competitors, or the company in question (see SWOT analysis!)

A strategy is more concerned with the "what" that needs to be accomplished.

The longer term goals are typically more strategic in nature. The shorter term goals are typically more tactical and specific to obtain a certain larger outcome.

Definition of tactical: small-scale actions serving a larger purpose, or adroit planning or maneuvering to accomplish a purpose.

As we work on shorter term goals, the tactical part becomes more about the "what and how." Fully developed, the short term goals will include the strategies of how to achieve, as well as details of the tasks that need to be completed. The best tactical plan is broken down to the week... ie:

"what needs to be done this week?"

f. MAKE IT BITE SIZE

The biggest error in most strategic business plans is that it is "too big" to execute.

I was invited into a business a few years ago where a "high dollar – big name" consultant had recently developed a very impressive two-binder strategic business plan for them. I am sure the consultant firm was very proud of this plan. The issue was this business did not even know where or how to start because it would take a PhD to understand it!

Consequently, I was hired to help boil it down for them and set them up on a step-by-step plan.

The old joke here is, "how do you eat an elephant?"

The age old answer...

So the same is true with goals and with a business plan.

MAKE. IT. BITE SIZE.

The goal is to break your goals and to do items in bite size chunks.

The truth is that you want a business plan that you can understand and execute. Another truth is that you have a business to run on a daily basis. Follow the k.i.s.s. rule here; Keep it simple stupid.

Chapter 2: Getting it Right-Setting the Foundation

Paramount's Plan for Success Process
Strategic Planning Made Easy.

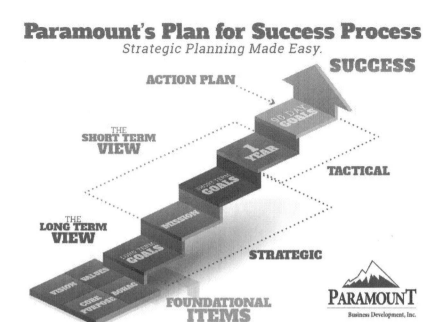

The key to business and to business planning is to set the right foundation. It is common knowledge that a house built on a poor foundation will not stand for long. The same is true for a business. It is critically important to get the foundation for a business right.

I often think about the rules of a sporting game when I think about this. For example, as I write this, the NCAA final four has just wrapped up. What makes this a great game is that the rules are simple and everyone knows them.

I consider setting the foundation for your business similar to the rules in a sporting game. For your players (employees) in this game (that we call business) it is important that they understand the rules of the game (foundation).

In the sections that follow, you will understand how to do this.

a. YOUR RULES OF THE GAME

Not long ago, a regional business, Wawa, distributed a book called "6 Core Values That Built a Business." While the book was simplistic, the meaning could not have been more important. When you run a business, everyone needs to know how you play the game of business.

For example, in my early career, I worked for a business owner whose most important core value was to make money. Anything you did, as long as you made money, was okay. Later on in my career, a CEO I worked for was more concerned about doing business in a high integrity and ethical way. A striking, and very important difference.

Even if you are new to business, I encourage you to set out your core values and how you want to run your business. This is not fluffy stuff. Do not be misled thinking this is obtuse, theoretical nonsense. This is important. It also may be a living, breathing, evolutional exercise. Don't expect it to be perfect and etched in stone in your first try. Over the years, you most likely will adjust and fine tune your core values.

The most important part of your core values is that it gives your employees guidance. In the absence of your personal presence, it gives them an idea on how you would make a decision if you were present. The other important part of your core values is that it gives your customer base a good idea of who you are. It will often make them feel more comfortable doing business with you.

However, a note of caution. Make sure the core values that you establish are what you will really follow and endeavor to live up to. If employees and customers see that you routinely do not run your business, and make your decisions along your core values, you will quickly be seen as a fraud and incongruent. Be sure your core values represent who you really are.

Many businesses that I go into have what I call pretty s_____ on the wall. While that <u>stuff</u> (what did you think s_____was referring to?) on their wall looks impressive and snazzy, it is for the most part, "lovely lies." No one knows it. No one follows it. No one cares. Not even the business owner/leader.

Please, if you are going to do this, and you must, make it real.

"If you don't stand for something,
You will fall for everything"

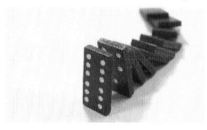

The best core value statements are 5 – 8 items/words, supported by a sentence or two of description. For an example, please visit our website. While you're there, go to http://paramountbusinessdevelopment.com/fsp-downloads and download an example of core value starter words.

b. WHY DOES YOUR COMPANY EXIST?

Establishing your core purpose is not an obvious step in business planning, but I can tell you from experience that it is a critical step. This, as all of your business plan, can change and evolve over time. In fact, I would expect it to. Your core purpose statement merely answers the simple question "what do you do?" In other words, as a business, "what is your core purpose?"

For example, Tom who runs the auto repair shop, his core purpose is:

"To fix and repair your late model vehicle and keep it in a safe, reliable, and running condition."

For him, he also includes a geographical area.

The reason for the core purpose is to keep you grounded and centered. Often, during running a business things come up that tend to pull you off track. For Tom, his core purpose statement keeps him centered on the mechanical and electrical repair of late model vehicles. It also keeps his team grounded and centered as well.

For a case in point, Tom told me that he was considering being a tire store. He was also thinking about getting his license to sell used cars to help out his friends. Today, the tire business is ruthless, with even internet sites selling tires. Also, in his case, there are 3 other tire dealers within 5 miles. Furthermore, to sell used cars effectively takes a big lot, and volume. Tom would have neither of these. Today, Tom's core purpose keeps him grounded and centered.

c. YOUR WHY

Part of setting a solid foundation is understanding why you do what you do. Why not cupcakes? Why not used cars? Why not lawn maintenance? Etc. The reason for the why is to keep you motivated in doing what you do, and to remind you, especially on the bad days!

For example, my why is to see business leaders succeed and reach a new level of success. Additionally, I hate to see business failure because I believe it is unnecessary. In the case of Tom, the auto mechanic, his why is simple. He grew up as a mechanic, he loves cars, he loves fixing cars, and he grew up in a family business. Tom's why is simply: "to continue the family business, and to continue my love of repairing cars for my friends and customers." This is a pretty easy task; probably one of the easiest of a business plan. You probably already know this intuitively. Put it down on paper!

d. VISION – REMEMBER THOSE BOUNDARIES!

One of the most exciting parts of business planning is setting your vision. This is sometimes the part that people struggle with the most, but there is no need to struggle!

Unfortunately, there are many purveyors of business services, namely business planning, and many books that have gotten this wrong. In turn, it has seeded much confusion. Many have confused and even switched the meaning of vision and mission. I like to keep things simple; the simpler the better.

Let's try this:

Vision: what you want to be when you grow up!

Mission: what you do, how you do it, and who you do it for.

It really is that simple.

So let's work on your vision.

The hardest question that I frequently get asked about vision is, "how far out into the future should my vision be?" That is a tough question and there is no perfect answer. My answer is to define that yourself for your purposes and your vision. For example, you may feel that a 10 year time period is appropriate. You may feel that the time frame of when you plan to retire is appropriate. Hey, I don't judge! It is your decision.

Going back to the most popular definition: what do you want to be when you grow up? First, pick a date. Next, try to envision what you would like your business to look like at that date. Let's use Tom the auto mechanic as an example.

In his earlier days, Tom showed up to work every day and just worked on cars. He was successful and growing. However, there was no compelling vision of the future. The plan was to get up tomorrow morning and do it again and that was basically it. It just became plain work.

After working with Tom over a few afternoons and pressing him to dream a little, he came up with a vision that was very motivating to him. Tom's vision was "to grow the best car repair business in my market and expand from 3 bays and 5 employees, to 7 bays and 10 employees, while becoming the 'go to' shop in my market."

This was really something Tom could wrap his head around and was very motivating to him. The fantastic part was that he did accomplish his vision in less than 10 years! Now his vision has changed and grown to either find a second shop nearby, or relocate his current shop where he can double in size. AGAIN.

A second bonus to Tom was that his new vision was extremely exciting and motivating to his team of mechanics. It gave them a pep in their step and a new way of looking at things.

A frequent question I often get asked is, "how do I determine my vision?" I usually recommend a quiet environment, a pizza, and 2 six-packs of beer!!! (kidding!!!) The serious answer is to find a chunk of time, a morning or afternoon, clear your desk, clear your mind, be uninterruptable, and dream a little! If you find this difficult, ask a good friend, or two, that you can brainstorm with to help you out.

After you have developed a trial vision, ask yourself:

Does it seem realistic?

Is it in line with my core purpose and my why?

Does it motivate me?

Will it motivate others?

Is it what I want?

Your vision will also change/grow/adjust over time. I believe what people find most challenging about this exercise is that they fear they will get it wrong. So what? What if you do? What is the worst thing that could happen? Again, you are able to change/grow/adjust your vision at any time that you deem it necessary.

Lastly, beware of "Vision Killers!" Vision Killers are items that extremely limit you, or limit your vision to standard, mundane, stereotypical items. Visions that are too short term are also duds. Visions with negative, defensive language are also no good. Remember that a good vision is to be inspiring and motivating.

VISION CASE STUDY: "Upward Energy Service"

A couple of years ago we were working with a 70+ year old energy services company. They provided heating oil, bioheat, and propane to their local market.

Throughout the years, they had continued to grow, mostly through acquisition. While they were in the energy services business, they really didn't do much in the heating equipment, or cooling equipment markets, mostly just providing heating fuels. They were actually missing opportunities in this area. Also, through their acquisitions, they were doing business under 4 different company names. And in some cases, they were competing with themselves!

The company owners, through the process of business planning, realized that they were really missing a main focus. In the bigger picture, they realized that they really lacked a motivating, inspiring vision for their company.

Several decisions had to be made here. Were they going to operate as one company, or were they going to operate as 4 autonomous companies? If they were going to focus more on heating/cooling equipment, was that going to be a 5th company; rolled into each company; or focused on by one, or more, of the companies?

I think it is obvious from this story that the issues were easily identifiable, and the benefits of having a strong vision is relatively obvious.

Through much thought and several meetings, the partners of the company decided on: (not verbatim)

- The parent company would be a "full service" energy services company including full HVAC maintenance and installation
- The other three companies would each focus on a particular style of business and/or a specific market segment
  - E.G.: one company was to focus on low price, low service heating fuels and be sold via the internet and prepaid purchases only
  - E.G.: the other two companies would each be very specifically focused on a target market and be mid-tier priced
- All four companies moving forward would be coordinated and run by the same administrative team, thus taking advantage of efficiencies and stripping out significant costs

Today Update: All four companies are doing exceptionally well and are much more profitable and focused.

e. WHAT'S A BOHAG?!

Okay. Wow. This is the easy one. Especially after you have determined your vision.

BOHAG: Big, Ole, Hairy, Audacious Goal

Big
Ole
Hairy
Audacious
GOAL

Again, in keeping it simple, I will offer an easy definition of a BOHAG. Given unlimited time, resources, and not holding back, what is your wildest dream that you would like to see your business accomplish?

Perhaps a couple of examples would help. My BOHAG is to help 10,000 business leaders find greater success and happiness in their business and to be the most sought after business/leadership coach in the mid-Atlantic region.

Tom's BOHAG is to grow his auto repair business into multiple locations in his region and to be the best auto repair chain. Period.

So this is really easy. What is yours? Have fun with this one!

f.   FOUNDATIONAL ITEMS PLANNING TOOL

Planning for your business is an arduous thoughtful process. To aid you in this work, we have created several simple tools to make it easier for you. Planning is enough work, who wants to develop all of the planning tools along with it???

For your convenience, we have created a tool to help you with these foundational items, including a tool for listing your goals.

Please go to:

http://paramountbusinessdevelopment.com/fsp-downloads

You will be asked for your email so that as we improve the tools, or create more, we can send them to you. Also, as we have Strategic Planning Conferences, we will let you know about those as well.

Chapter 3: SWOT Analysis: The Free, Invaluable Tool

S W O T !

STRENGTHS	WEAKNESSES
OPPORTUNITIES	**THREATS**

Wow. This is such a huge, sensitive topic. Not to rain on my professional colleagues' parades, but too much is made of this topic. I am not saying this is not an extremely important topic, or an important part of business planning. I am, however, saying that many of my professional colleagues make this part of planning too complicated. Way too complicated.

A SWOT Analysis is an easy task but a lot of thought needs to be put into it. And to be useful, there may even need to be some research on your customers' opinions, your market, and your competitors to effectively complete this task. As a business owner/leader you should be in relatively good touch with all of this already. However, some of you may not be. Also, many professional colleagues, and even some books that have been written, get the SWOT analysis all wrong. There are two simple rules to follow to keep your SWOT analysis useful and effective:

1: Strengths and Weaknesses are to be **internal** to your company. Opportunities and Threats are to be **external** to your company. No exceptions. Period. Simple rule, but often misunderstood and not applied.

2: Please do not be sophomoric and make strengths and weaknesses just simple opposites of each other. Similarly, do not make opportunities and threats opposites of each other. What is the value of doing this? E.G. do not make a "good economy" an opportunity and a "bad economy" a threat.

A SWOT analysis has to be done before doing any goal setting, as this needs to be a precursor to determining what goals would be effective and meaningful for your business. My simple example above about a good or bad economy would most likely have a direct impact on the goals you would set for your company going forward. Providing you know your customers, market, and competitors, a thorough SWOT analysis could be completed in well under 4 hours. Amazingly, some purveyors of this service schedule 2-3 day retreats, and charge tens of thousands of dollars for this. Amazing!

Strengths

The first section to complete in a SWOT analysis is the strengths. Please remember that the strengths are internal to your company. Making a list of your strengths should be strengths that are important to either your customers, your company, or your market, or strengths that add uniqueness to you when compared to your competitors.

Don't just say simple, vague things like "I have a good team." There's really very little meaning in that statement. However, you might make a statement that says I have a team that, on average, has 15 years of experience which is at least 5 years more than my best competitor. Other strengths could be things like unique products, unique marketing strategies, maybe faster delivery times, and the list goes on. But the main point to remember while doing your strengths is if they somehow are significant to your customers, your market, or when compared to your competitors. If they are not significant, then they are not a true strength.

Weaknesses

Please remember that when completing a section on your weaknesses, do not make these simply the opposites of your strengths. There really is not much value in that. However, these weaknesses should be a very brutally honest assessment of the weak points within your company. Maybe you have a particularly weak customer service department. Maybe your guarantees are weak. Perhaps you have an inferior product compared to your competitors. Again, you should be taking the viewpoint as it relates to your customers, your market, and your competitors. Customer surveys and competitor analyses can be very helpful with this exercise.

When doing your strengths and weaknesses, this should be a brainstorming session that you either do by yourself, or one that you do with yourself and your top managers. The important part here is to make it a brainstorming session, not a session where people are trying to win an argument, or prove a point. None of that is important. However, being explanatory and saying what you mean is important. After completing the strengths and weaknesses, you should go back and prioritize the top five from each list.

Opportunities

The point of opportunities is to assess your company and its position within your market, and to determine what opportunities may be in the market that could be important to the further development of your company. These may be opportunities that relate to new customers, your existing customer base, your market, expanding your product line, or maybe even to exploit your competitors. Again, please remember this is external to your company.

For example, you might have an opportunity to introduce a new product to your product line that your customers have already identified as something they would want and be happy if you provided it.

Another example could be that you have a competitor who is weak at marketing a certain segment of the product line or service line to a particular target market. This may open up an opportunity for you to drive new sales in a new market for your company.

Assessing the opportunities could possibly be the most important part of your SWOT analysis. In a recent client example, the company had innovated and created a "new design take" on a very standard, common product. In displaying this new design, there was significant customer interest. Therefore, there was a new opportunity to market and produce this "new design" product. So far in 2018, this has led to over $90,000 in new sales.

Threats

When assessing the threats to your company, it really is important to understand your customers, your market, and especially your competitors. As a Business Coach, I often come upon companies that say they don't care what their competitors do and don't pay attention to their competitors. This is an especially dangerous view to take. My advice is to always keep an eye on your competitors to see how they may be changing or morphing themselves to address your market, and your customer base. By watching your competitors often, you can identify threats to your business in plenty of time to take appropriate action. Similarly, if you're not watching your competitors you can often get badly surprised at the last moment when it might be too late to take appropriate action.

I am often asked why I focus on the privately, or closely held business market. The answer is simple. Agility. I worked for large multi-national corporations for over 20 years. Even the most straight-forward, no nonsense decisions often take months. As a private business, your most valuable business advantage is often agility-the ability to make a speedy business decision and quickly pivot, if needed. Use this to your advantage when necessary.

Wrapping It All Up

When you are all done with the SWOT analysis, you should end up with five strengths, weaknesses, opportunities, and threats. These five should be the most important ones that you have identified, by priority.

Depending on the planning frequency that you establish for your company, and I recommend at least yearly, if not quarterly, you will want to update this SWOT analysis each time. The SWOT analysis is a dynamic assessment of your entire customer base, your market, your company, and your competitors.

A successfully completed SWOT analysis will be critical to helping you select the appropriate goals to drive business success going forward. Please don't skip this step, but don't obsess about it and make it a 2 to 4 day project either. Typically, I have found that the things that come to your mind first, are the most significant things.

SWOT ANALYSIS CASE STUDY: "Excellent Door Company"

Business planning should never be done without a SWOT analysis. A properly executed SWOT analysis will usually set the basic framework for completing your business planning. Oftentimes, a business owner will go about the day-to-day work of running his/her business without looking at the whole big picture.

Several years ago, while working with the owner of a door company, we were facing huge changes in his market. For many years, the main part of his business was installing new doors in new homes that were under construction. His company was the sub-contractor for builders building new homes.

The new construction market had dropped off precipitously due to the financial crisis of the 2008 – 2010 time frame. The company's gross revenue had also dropped off precipitously. While doing a SWOT analysis, several items became obvious.

His company and his crews were really good at installing doors. From a customer service point of view, his crews got high ratings. His product line, that was one of the best in the industry, was very well received and got a high satisfaction rating in the market. However, due to the economy, his business was off and it was clear that there was no immediate sign of a return.

Through this cold, hard splash in the face as a result of the SWOT analysis, it was obvious that the business would not survive if significant changes were not made.

In reviewing a very well done SWOT analysis, the correct strategy moving forward was identified. The company decided to focus on maintenance and retro-fits for the residential market. They had always done this work, but due to their focus on the new home builders, they had never focused on this market segment.

Thus, their new opportunity become the residential retro-fit and maintenance market. They went after this market with a do-or-die zeal.

Months later, it worked. Thankfully. This strategy saved the company and was born out of a strong SWOT analysis.

Today Update: This Company, 8 years later, continues to grow and be successful. The new home market has still not fully recovered but thanks to a well done SWOT analysis, this company has thrived.

Chapter 4: Planning for the Long Term

A common question is "how long is long term?" Good question. I will focus on that in a bit. I want to remind you of the process here. We are starting with the long term view of your business. With each step of this planning, we are breaking it down into shorter time horizons. Your first steps were to set your business foundation. While these items may get adjusted over time, we consider these your "forever" items:

Core values

Core purpose

Why

Vision

BOHAG

Now it is time to start breaking this down into shorter and shorter time frames.

a. HOW LONG ARE WE TALKIN' HERE?

What is the proper long term horizon? Highly valuable question. And now for my highly valuable answer: "It depends!"

Okay. So now you are ready to start throwing darts at me...

What time frame did you set for your vision? Your long term goals should be something less than that. When I first started helping clients with business planning, I recommended using 10 – 30 years as a "long term" horizon. Unfortunately, that was a mistake. I don't know about you, but my crystal ball is no good out to that time frame! In determining your vision, my guidance typically is the 10 – 15 year range. That is, unless you have a more relevant time frame for you specifically, or your business.

Today, my guidance for long term goal planning is 3- 5 years. While that may seem short, I guide clients in that direction because most of us can wrap our head around that time frame. 10 – 30 years is too long. There are way too many unknowns in that length of time. There are already plenty of unknowns in the 3 – 5 year time frame!

Some of the unknowns are things like:

> The economy
> The market shifts
> New innovative products and services
> The competitive market
> Competitors
> Disruptions

And I could fill the rest of the book with the unknowns but I believe you get the picture.

b. THE DIFFERENCE BETWEEN LONG TERM & SHORT TERM

The concept of long term vs. short term goes back to "start with the end in mind" and back down from there. Remember "make it bite size?"

So in this context, we want to start with the vision and BOHAG. Then reduce it down to simply long term; specifically down to 3-5 years. You choose.

The next step is to break that down further into short term goals – specifically 1 year. And then break it down even further. We recommend 90 days. However, in your business, you may choose to break it down into seasons. Many businesses have seasons. Sometimes the seasons correlate to weather seasons. Sometimes they correlate down to busy season and slow season.

Some examples might be a landscaping company which usually will further break down their annual goals into winter/spring season, and summer/fall season. Heating fuel companies have a winter season, and a summer season. So on and so forth.

What shorter time frames work best for your company?

To keep things simple, we usually just stick to 90 days, or the standard quarters; Q1, Q2, Q3, and Q4.

Another point, while on this subject, is to similarly align your financial statements and other record keeping with these short term cycles. This is also why we prefer Q1, Q2, Q3, and Q4. Your bankers and CPA will prefer seeing your financials based on standard quarterly periods.

Another note: Sometimes the annual cycle of a business, AKA the fiscal year, does not match the calendar year. This is often true for C Corporations, or even other companies that base their books on specific seasonal cycles. In our case throughout this book, we will discuss annual goals, annual planning, etc., assuming your annual "cycle" matches the calendar year. If your fiscal year is different than the calendar year, please adjust the time based comments in this book accordingly.

c. STAY TRUE TO YOUR VISION & CORE PURPOSE

During the section on "making it bite size," we mentioned congruency. As you break down your goals, or "chunk them down" from your vision and your BOHAG, you need to remember to stay congruent.

It makes absolutely no sense to create goals at any time period that are at odds with your vision and BOHAG. Let's say, for example, that you want to expand into an adjacent geographical market to the west in order to grow your sales and your regional dominance. If this was part of your vision, why would you make a short term goal to buy a friend's company two states away? While that company might be a fine company, and buying it might help out your friend, how does it fit into your long range plan? The congruency aspect is another reason to "start with the end in mind."

Earlier, we discussed one planning method that started with the short term and built it up into long term goals. This makes no sense. That is like saying, "I am going to build a house with no plans, and I am just going to start by building a stand-alone bathroom!" (I think that is called an outhouse, and I have never heard of building a house starting with an outhouse!)

Another crucial area of congruency is within your core purpose. One of the reasons it is important to establish your core purpose is to establish boundaries. In my example of Tom, the mechanic, his core purpose is "to fix and repair your late model vehicle and keep it in safe, reliable, running condition." For Tom, keeping his goals congruent with his core purpose guides him to keep his goals within the context of growing, improving, and expanding his repair shop. A goal of establishing tire sales at his repair shop would be incongruent and pull his energy, time, and capital away from growing his core business.

Keep it congruent!

d. WRITE OUT YOUR LONG TERM GOALS, ALL OF THEM

My guidance for long term goal planning is 3- 5 years. Start with your vision and your BOHAG in mind and chunk these down to the 3 – 5 year time frame.

So in Tom's vision, he wants to be the best independent car repair shop in his county and wants to have multiple locations. Today, he simply has one repair shop. If his vision is to be #1 in the county with several shops, what should be his goal in the 3-5 year time frame? To have 2? To have 4?

Some ideas for additional goals for that time frame might be to:

- Develop processes to run additional locations
- Invest in a computer system including service operation software, accounting software, and key performance indicator tracking; all for management purposes
- Develop leaders to be shop managers of additional locations
- Develop relationships with lenders to provide the necessary financing

I hope this gives you some ideas for how to proceed with the long term goals.

The main idea is to start with your vision and BOHAG and break it down to doable steps in the long frame time period.

The key is to keep these long term goals relevant and congruent with your vision and BOHAG.

As you do this step, it is okay to come up with many goals. Let the ideas flow in free form. The bigger term for this is brainstorming.

After you have completed a long list of 3 – 5 year goals, the next step is to prioritize them. For goal setting purposes, I strongly recommend narrowing it down to your top 5 goals, or less. And prioritize those top 5 so that you know which one is the most important, down to number 5.

So you may have had 10-15 goals and now you have narrowed it down to 5. And now panic sets in. "But what do I do about the other 5 – 10 goals I identified?!"

Read on.

e. THE PARKING LOT-KEEPING IDEAS STORED FOR LATER

The Parking Lot

	BFO	Relevance	$ Value	Quarter	Description
1.					
2.					
3.					
4.					
5.					
6.					
7.					
8.					
9.					
10.					
11.					
12.					
13.					
14.					

So, Tom's business can lend us a great metaphor for all of the goals that did not make the top 5 based on priority.

In Tom's business when they get more business than they can handle, they simply just put the additional cars to fix out in the parking lot. When do they bring them in? When they get some of the others done and have the space and the labor to work on them.

We have developed a parking lot form for you convenience: Go to: http://paramountbusinessdevelopment.com/fsp-downloads to download and save yourself time.

Through the quarter, and throughout the year, you will often accomplish your goals before their deadline. Sometimes the goals will be easier to attain than you thought. Sometimes your team will be fired up and achieve things faster than you imagined possible. I believe in limiting the goals that you are focusing on to 5 or less. With too many goals, you will get overwhelmed and a sense of lack of accomplishment.

When you do end up accomplishing goals before their deadline, now is the time to go to the parking lot and pull up the next highest priority goal and start working on it. Sometimes leaders are loath to do this because they feel they will not be able to complete them in the remaining time they have left in the quarter. So what?

If they do not get done by the end of the quarter, simply roll them over into the next quarter. The main thing is that you are continuing to get things checked off and still making progress!

Also, by keeping a parking lot list, no great goals (thoughts at this stage) will ever be lost. So you will have a parking lot list for your long range (3-5 year) goals, short term (1 year) goals, and quarterly goals.

Further, on a quarterly basis, review the parking lot to be sure that the items on there from before are still relevant and valid. It serves no purpose to have a burgeoning parking lot full of old nonsense.

Keeping a vibrant and meaningful parking lot is highly valuable. As you select your next quarter's goals, the parking lot is one of the first things you should check. Having a healthy, well-defined parking lot is a great tool for a business.

Chapter 5: Planning for the Short Term

As we discussed earlier, there is a difference between the long term and short term views. Earlier we defined the long term view as 3- 5 years. So what is the short term view?

We define the short term view for the purposes of planning as 1 year, and as quarters. E.G. Q1, Q2, Q3 and Q4. Also, 1 year will typically be defined as January 1st through December 31st. As we go further in this book, we will use this context for short term.

Depending on your business, you may have significant reason for using different time periods. For example, for the 1 year, or annual plan, you may have a fiscal year that is different than the calendar year. In this case, please use your fiscal year.

Also, depending on your business, you may want to define your shorter timeframes based on something that is unique and meaningful to your business specifically. See the earlier section that explained this further under "what is the proper horizon."

a. 1 YEAR – SHORT TERM GOALS

The next step in planning is to develop your 1 year goals, or annual goals. To begin this, start with your long term goals. As you think about developing your company toward your vision, you are continuing to "chunk it down" to bite size pieces that are digestible within the time frame. In this case, one year.

As you did with the long term goals, start by listing all of the goals that you think of that will need to be accomplished in the next year to move you closer to your long term goals.

Let's consider Tom and his auto repair business. His goal is to be the best independent car repair shop in his region, and to have multiple locations. Today, he simply has one repair shop. He decided his long term goals were to:

- Add 2 – 4 additional locations
- Develop processes to run additional locations
- Invest in a computer system, including service operation software, accounting software, and key performance indicator tracking; all for management purposes
- Develop leaders to be shop managers of additional locations
- Develop relationships with lenders to provide the necessary financing

Obviously these are large goals that will have to be broken down into small chunks to accomplish in one year. Some of his annual goals could be:

- Find a car repair business in an adjacent location to acquire
- Develop a daily close out procedure for handling cash, checks, and credit card slips
- Find a better service operation software to aid in running his business and multiple locations
- Start to develop John, his shop foreman, to be the general manager of his current location
- Grow sales by 20% at the current location
- Grow net profit by 25% at the current location
- Etc. Etc.

In his case, Tom developed a total of 17 goals for the 1 year time frame. A lot of goals!

Just as in the case with the long term goals, the next task is ….. you guessed it – to prioritize the top 5 goals and put them in their proper order 1 through 5.

Depending on the complexity and size of the goals, 5 may not be the appropriate number. It is better to have 3 goals that can be reasonably accomplished in 1 year than to have 5 goals that become overwhelming.

Again, as before, put the rest of the goals in the 1 year parking lot. This step is especially critical at the one year level and again at the 90 day level.

b. BE SMART ABOUT THOSE GOALS

Specific Measurable Achievable Results Timeframe

SMART

G O A L S

Have you heard of SMART goals? Have you been setting SMART goals?

Most beginning efforts of strategic planning fail due to not setting SMART style goals. For the vision, BOHAG and long term goals, SMART style goals are not necessary, and in most cases, not desirable. However, once we move into short term goals, annual, and 90 day goals, the SMART format is mandatory.

As the graphic illustrates, SMART format goals are pretty straight-forward. There is really no smoke and mirrors, or magic. In fact, the SMART format makes pure, simple sense.

S = specific. The short term goals need to be specific, meaning they are well described and not vague or ambiguous. For goals to be meaningful, they need to be clear and easily understood.

In Tom's example, it is very clear what the long term goal of "add 2-4 additional locations" means. To make this an appropriate short term goal, it needs to be more specific. An example would be: "Identify one additional location."

M = measurable. Measurable means that the goal needs to be quantifiable, or stated in such a way that it is easy to measure. For example, if we said we want to "increase sales" as an annual goal, it would not be a measurable goal. However, if we restated it, and said we want to "increase sales by 15%" it is now measurable.

In Tom's example of "add 2-4 additional locations" it is easily measurable. It would be better if his goal was more specific and said "add 2 additional locations." In this case, it is more precise and exact.

A = achievable. Often, companies have goals that are not achievable. Because they are not achievable in the short term, they become unmotivating and discouraging. I believe this is one reason why some companies start and then abandon business planning.

We could debate what is achievable all day long. Especially when you read news accounts of other companies achieving amazing things like doubling sales revenue in 1 year. Making goals achievable is a tricky thing and you have to know yourself and your company. Is it reasonable to set a goal of doubling sales in one year? I would suggest to you that it is not achievable for most companies.

A long time ago, I had a boss that loved to make us set what he called "stretch goals." His idea was to set the goals high enough that you had to work really hard to achieve them. So the debate was always "how much of a stretch is too much?" Unfortunately in his case, he often forced them to be set so high they became too high and unachievable. This became unmotivating and discouraging.

I strongly believe in setting goals that you believe you can achieve. Steady progress is better than no progress.

R = results oriented. Goals that are set for your company should be results oriented. By this I mean that they should matter to your end results. If you set goals unrelated to the results of the business, many bad things can happen. They can become a wild goose chase, a diversion, a waste of time, etc.

The best way to keep goals results oriented is to make sure they are in alignment with your longer term goals. Please remember that goals should roll up, or trickle down, and all be in good congruency with where and how you want your company to grow.

T = time based. Because you are setting one year and 90 day goals, they are time based by de facto. However, an annual goal could have a completion date of something different than 12/31/xx. It could have a completion date of 6/30/xx or 10/1/xx. The same is true for the 90 day goals. Often my clients have goals that are set to be completed by 1/31/xx. The idea behind the time based goals is to keep things moving forward and to develop momentum. Goals without deadlines are just dreams.

c. THE DIFFERENCE BETWEEN GOALS & TASKS

Many people become confused between goals and tasks. Most of the business leaders that I have met with readily say that they have goals. However, upon a closer look at their list of "goals," I find that it really is a list of 15 or so tasks.

When I try to explain the difference, most people become confused or resistant to the idea that a goal and a task are different.

So let's rely on our friend, *"the Webster dictionary:"*

Definition of goal: the end toward which effort is directed.

Definition of task: a usually assigned piece of work often to be finished within a certain time.

In my explanation of goals and tasks, I usually refer to a goal as the end result of something we are trying to accomplish. After we set goals, we will want to determine a strategy, or strategies, that we will use to accomplish the goal. Then, there are often a list of tasks that we will need to follow to complete the strategy(ies), and eventually accomplish the goal.

A great example is the goal of Harry to modernize his plant and have computerized controls throughout to increase production and quality. As a manufacturing plant of over 100 people, this was a major undertaking.

Harry's long range goal was to have all major processes in his manufacturing plant to be under computerized controls. His annual goal was to begin in the batching part of his plant where the process began.

His theory was to control the raw materials going into his manufacturing plant as the first step to better output quality.

So, to accomplish getting the computerization of the batching operation, there were many strategies to follow first. They first had to decide their priorities for the computerization. Then they had to select a vendor; then there was the specific design of the system to meet their specific needs, and so on.

Each of the above strategies were detailed out to include many tasks and sub tasks. The one goal of computerizing the batching operation became quite the detailed project with dozens of tasks. However, the tasks were just tasks; just part of the overall goal.

In Harry's case, with this one goal being such a large undertaking, Harry wisely limited the number of other goals that his organization was pursuing during this time period.

d. MISSION-WHAT IS IT?

I start this section somewhat reluctantly. I believe too much is made of a mission(s) statement.

For clarity, I believe there are two different kinds of "mission" statements. The first is the overall clarifying one at the company level. The second one is used to define a current mission at a lower, short length of time level.

Please let me explain. First, as I said earlier, many get the mission and the vision statements confused. Many professionals who help businesses even get this confused!

At an overall company level, a mission statement is really pretty simple. It describes 3 things:

- Who are we?
- What do we do?
- And who do we do it for?

Yes, it is that simple. At the organization level, if you have completed the vision statement, BOHAG, core purpose, and why, the mission statement can feel a little redundant. It is. That is why I often do not make a big deal about it.

In our example of Tom Shim, he completed a mission statement for his business:

"We are a trustworthy, helpful, friendly, independent auto repair shop doing mechanical repairs on late model automobiles and light trucks in the Monroe County area."

This mission statement succinctly sums up Tom's repair shop and makes it very clear to all what his company is all about.

The positives for a mission statement is that they do just that. And they keep the company anchored and on a controlled path.

Mission(s) statements are also commonly used to describe large initiatives. A good example of this was when the U.S. military dubbed the first Iraqi war "Desert Storm," and the second one "Desert Shield."

When used in this context, mission statements can be very focusing and fun. Consider our example of Tom and his repair shop business. Let's say he moved up the goal of buying a 2nd location across town. Just imagine all the individual tasks that would be needed to make this large goal successful. A very positive step in creating this whole big goal would be to give it a catchy name.

A catchy name would give the project an identity. The name would also pull in and motivate the team. And it quite possibly could add to its chances of success.

For Tom's purposes, he decides to give his mission of establishing a 2nd location a name. He now calls it "Operation West Side Invasion!"

Chapter 6: The Tactical Plan

a. REMEMBER TO STAY CONGRUENT

90 days goals are simply just that. They are the goals broken down from your annual goals that you need to achieve in 90 days. Throughout this book, we have stressed the need to be congruent. While a 90 day goal does not have to be a subset of an annual goal, it surely needs to be congruent with the long term and annual goals. Otherwise, what is the point?

Let's refer back to Harry's annual goal to computerize his batching operation at his manufacturing plant.

In January, Harry set the goal to have his batching operation computerized. This is where his manufacturing process starts. Harry's idea is to follow the old "garbage in – garbage out" mantra. By computerizing his batch operation, his theory is that if he can provide a better quality infeed of batched raw materials, the output quality of his manufacturing operation will improve.

Computerizing his batching operations is a large goal. While he does not yet know the exact investment, he is guessing it will be over $1 million and will take a 30 day period to get fully installed and operational.

So, as part of setting the annual goal, Harry has broken this annual goal down into steps. He determined that the appropriate goal for the 1st quarter was to go out to the known vendors and solicit designs and quotes for this project. He further determined that he would take all the quotes, evaluate them, and make a design and vendor decision in the 2nd quarter.

So the chunked down 1st quarter goal was to go to the vendors and solicit designs and quotes. However, this goal was broken down into several pieces.

For example, the first smaller goal was to determine the output quality parameters of the batching operations. These parameters would then be given to the vendors as baseline requirements.

Another smaller goal was to review the equipment vendors' market to ensure that they had a list of all of the relevant vendors to solicit quotes from.

Yet a third smaller goal, estimating the project to cost $1 million, was to consider how this project would be paid for. For example: out of retained earnings, traditional bank loan, additional paid in capital from stockholders, etc.

And there were additional sub goals that Harry developed for the 1st quarter that were supportive and congruent with the larger annual goal.

While one year to accomplish this task may seem like a long time, there are many steps to this (as there is with many goals) **and** Harry and his team had an ongoing, demanding, business to run on a daily basis!

When you are selecting and making your list of 90 day goals, please remember that it is only ***90 days!*** Please do not fall into the trap of selecting 10, 15 or more goals. Remember that you only have 90 days, and meanwhile you have a company to run on a daily basis. Our strict guidance is no more than 5 goals. Preferably 3-4.

At this point many business owners reach a state of panic and say:

I can't cut it down to 5 or less!

But I have so many things that I need to get done!

How can I possibly prioritize these?

What do I do with the others if I cut it down to only 5?

We hear these complaints or admonitions all the time. Rarely in our experience does a company ever accomplish 5 goals in a quarter. What is better? To have 5 goals and get frustrated with the enormity of it and get none done, or to have 3 goals and comfortably and confidently get all 3 done?

Think about it. If you consistently can get 3, or more, goals completed a quarter, you will have improved your business at the end of the year by completing 12 or more goals! I suggest to you that will be better than 95% of your competitors!

Additionally, if you have more than 5 goals, you remember where the rest of them go... right? The parking lot!

Finally, as it pertains to prioritization, we recommend that the 3 – 5 goals that you have for the 90 days, you put in priority order. Then plan your strategies and tasks accordingly. Work on the most important goal first.

b. KEEP IT ROLLIN'

So when I think of this topic, the old Aerosmith song, "Train Kept a Rollin" comes to mind. I have often met business leaders that complete business plans for their business and then do not act on them. Why? They "did not have time!"

I will submit to you that doing a business plan, and then not acting on it, is a poor waste of time. So how do we keep it rolling?

We have developed a weekly activity chart http://paramountbusinessdevelopment.com/fsp-downloads to combat this lethargy or lack of activity.

Quarterly Goals - in priority order:

Goals	Actions/Strategies	Who	When - start	When - Finish	Wk 1	Wk 2	Wk 3	Wk 4	Wk 5	Wk 6	Wk 7	Wk 8	Wk 9	Wk 10	Wk 11	Wk 12	Wk 13
Goal #1:																	
Goal #2:																	
Goal #3:																	
Goal #4:																	
Goal #5:																	

The last piece of 90 day planning is to schedule out the tasks on a weekly basis. Who will do what, by when? Notice "who" is in that statement. Yes! If necessary, you need to assign specific tasks to specific individuals. As the leader of a business, it is doubtful that you will do every task!

Part of this step should be a team meeting to present the 90 day plan to your top team to create awareness among them and get buy in to the plan. Ideally, you would have derived the 90 day plan with this team.

To keep the plan rolling, there should be a periodic meeting to update progress and to refine the task list going forward. In most businesses that are serious about their plan, this a short weekly meeting with the top team.

By having a continuous focus on the plan, and having periodic status update meetings, the level of focus on the plan stays high, and progress is held in high accountability.

Keep. It. Rollin'.

c. PUTTING IT ALL TOGETHER!

By now you have a lot of notes and a lot of paper. You are probably wondering how you are going to keep all of this neat, organized, and easily useful.

To that end, we have created, and continued to refine, a one page summary for strategic planning purposes. All of your notes and details will not fit on this one page.

Go to:

http://paramountbusinessdevelopment.com/fsp-downloads to download your copy of the one page plan.

The purpose of this one page plan is to include "just enough" detail that it reminds you of your foundational items and your goals. Once you have reached this point, you will want to transfer the high level details to this one page.

The best use of this one page plan is to keep it in a visible location. Hang it on the wall, put it under a clear desk mat, etc.

The point is to refer to it frequently to keep you reminded of your plan and to hold yourself accountable and continue to move things forward.

d. WHEN TO JUMP OFF OF YOUR HORSE!

So it has been reported that in the old days of a battle, one of the most important things was to learn when to "get off of your horse!" When it is dead of course!

Okay, so maybe a bad old joke, but the point is: when do you toss away a goal?

Sometimes business leaders become so beholden to a goal that they ruin their companies pursuing it, or they pursue a bad goal to huge damaging costs.

A business owner once told me that they had garbage cans and dumpsters full of bad ideas that had gone nowhere. He said wisdom was knowing when to stop! IE: Get off your horse if it is dead!

Yes, sometimes we select goals that upon further learning, or changes in the market, or economy, or one of many factors, they become bad goals. So drop the goal. Delete it. Forget about it. Just stop it!

The wisdom is knowing when to discard a goal. IT IS OKAY to admit that things have changed, or we have learned that this goal is no longer important to our future success.

Chapter 7: Critical, But Often Forgotten

Often in the high pursuit of business goals, there are many categories and items that possibly get left behind. A lot of these items include professional learning, individual development plans, mentoring, team development, performance recognition, and the list goes on.

The important thing here is to look at the whole business when we do strategic business planning. The most often forgotten parts are the "soft" side of the business – the people part.

A non-people part that is often not considered is the systems of the business, and the IT/software part of the business.

Be sure to look at everything during planning.

a. POSSIBLY THE MOST IMPORTANT PART

Possibly the most important part of business planning is working on you!

Are you the Leader your business needs?

Are you the person you need to **_"BE"_** to lead and execute this plan?

Personal, self-development is a serious topic. This is a good place for everyone to stop, look in the mirror, and calmly evaluate themselves. And answer these questions:

> Who do I need to be to successfully lead and execute my business plan?

> How should I invest in myself?

> What do I need to learn?

> How do I need to grow?

> What do I need to learn to execute my business plan?

> What outside resources can I bring in to help?

It is often tragic to see that business leaders have neglected to invest in themselves and grow. As you are reading this you are probably thinking I am talking about older leaders, i.e. over 55 years old. This is not true. I have seen it occur at all age groups and it is based on what I call the "I Know it All" Disease.

Tom has a goal of expanding his auto repair business into multiple locations. Tom knows that he will have to learn how to run multiple locations. As a very hands-on person, he is very concerned about this because he knows that he cannot be in more than one place at one time.

After much contemplation, Tom decided to invest in himself to learn how to lead and manage multiple locations at one time. He also knew that he needed to understand staffing multiple locations and having the systems for controlling cash, customer satisfaction, etc. In Tom's case, he decided to invest in business and executive coaching, and increased services from his CPA and attorney.

Remember that there is no point in developing a great business plan that you cannot execute.

CASE STUDY: "The Family Manufacturing Company"

We began working with a 3rd generation manufacturing company about 4 years ago. The manufacturing company was a well-run, well respected company in their market. Coming off of the 2008-2010 financial crisis, their team environment was relatively stable.

As the market began to heat up in the 2016-2018 time frame, several stresses and strains started to become evident. Also during this time frame, the employment market started to heat up. Finding manufacturing plant workers and delivery drivers was beginning to get more and more difficult.

Through successive business planning cycles, it became apparent to the leadership team that the team atmosphere, the leadership structure, and skill of the leadership team was becoming more and more important.

The leadership team began a structure of many team meetings and a more thorough planning of the atmosphere of the work place, the players on the leadership team, and their leadership skills.

The careful focus of the team meetings was mainly to communicate the current status of initiatives, the current focus on the leaders, and to reinforce the established company values and vision.

The organization structure was changed and higher skilled leaders were brought into key positions. The top leaders spent a considerable amount of time with the leadership team to be sure their individual leadership was congruent to the company values, vision, and current plan.

Meanwhile, the top two leader/partners began investing in themselves significantly to grow their leadership skills in the right direction. They each began one-on-one leadership coaching, including beginning to read leadership articles and books and assuming local non-profit leadership roles.

Today Update: Today in 2018, the unemployment rate is about 3.7%; reported to be the lowest in 49 years. CDL drivers are reportedly impossible to hire. Yet this company, today, has potential employees coming to them wanting to be on their team!!! Why??? Because the word is out. They are a good employer with a good environment that empowers their people and are great people to work with and for. They pay average, or slightly above average, wages.

The top leaders are confident and capable. This is a leadership team that is humble, cooperative, and encouraging. They also expect great customer service and great customer results. There is little or no drama within this company.

b. ALL HANDS ON DECK

So, the plan is all complete. You have determined what your self-development will be over the next 90 days. Now what?

We have found that the best business plans are fully communicated to the entire team. Every player in the game needs to know the game plan (business plan!)

By now, hopefully you have already involved your top team and they have totally bought into the business plan for the quarter.

So what is the next step?

If you were the captain of a 1100s Viking ship, you would surely want everyone rowing toward the same goal. It is no different in business. Let's get all the team members working on your business plan. And yes, every member has a part to play.

The best way to inform every one of the business plan is to have an all hands on deck meeting. This is a great way to kick off a new quarter and a new quarterly business plan. Make it a team event with the idea of communicating the entire plan for the purpose of inclusion of all team members.

Here is a great simplified agenda for this meeting:

- o Review the results and accomplishments of last quarter's business plan
- o Review business accomplishments (non plan items) of last quarter

- Celebrate your wins!
- Give out awards to those whose input and hard work were instrumental in achieving your goals – if appropriate. (Remember, leaders who show their humility and spread praise and elevate others gain commitment and respect from their peers and subordinates)
- Thank them for their hard work and participation – make it meaningful
- Announce the next quarter's goals and why each one is significant. Tie it into your why and your vision

c. SO POWERFUL AND COSTS NOTHING!

In a prior section, we touched on the idea of having an "all hands on deck" meeting to wrap up the outgoing quarter's goals and introduce the new quarter's incoming goals. We also briefly mentioned gratitude and acknowledgement as part of the meeting.

Gratitude and acknowledgement are some of the most powerful people tools ever. Let's be straight. Everyone enjoys receiving gratitude and getting acknowledged for a job well done. Even you!

Praise is powerful, and it actually costs nothing. Nothing.

Team celebrations are a powerful way to thank and acknowledge a whole team. My findings over a long time is that employees love to eat, they love to party, and they love to kick back and socialize. I have also found that a team that "plays" together, "stays" together and outperforms other teams.

During team celebrations, this is the perfect time to sincerely and specifically express gratitude and acknowledge individuals who have gone above and beyond and made special commitments.

Elevating individuals, while possibly embarrassing to them at the moment, will present model behavior for others to follow and emulate. The other secret is, while possibly embarrassing the individual at the moment, especially a private and/or humble person, they will cherish that moment forever and most likely work even harder in the future.

This book is not specifically about how to reward teams and how to reward individuals. There have been many books about these topics before. Read them. Study them. Execute well!

Just do it!

If you are doubtful about this section, ask yourself one question...

> "Will my team perform better, or worse, in the future if I express my gratitude and acknowledgement for a job well done?"

Chapter 8: One Simple Truth

Wow. After all of this coach, how can I possibly kick it up another notch?

Well, let's talk about that!

In over 20 years of running businesses, and over a dozen years of coaching businesses, I have proved one simple truth:

Businesses that plan, succeed and outperform their peers.

Why? Because over 90%+ of the privately owned businesses do not do business planning.

By initiating and starting down the path of business planning, you have already put yourself in the minority of all businesses out there. Thus, you will outperform them.

So, how do you kick it up another notch?

1) As a beginner at business planning, do not become discouraged.
2) Plan the work, and work the plan. Push through it.
3) Start modestly. Start with a few goals.
4) Make planning a part of your daily/weekly ritual.
5) Keep "the train a rollin'." I.e.: stay focused on continual business planning.

It has been proven in study after study that businesses that do business planning outperform. I guarantee that over a 3 year period you will begin seeing results that you could have never imagined in the past.

EPILOGUE

THE REST OF THE STORY

"Within a few weeks" comes pretty fast. As their last meeting was around the Thanksgiving holidays, the brothers ended up meeting again just before the Christmas holidays. Tom, Dick and Harry had each done their due diligence and came back to the family dinner with ideas, names, and contacts. Dick and Harry had even interviewed a couple of people.

Their discussion on the porch was quite fruitful. They all came to the conclusion that they needed to have someone help them set up a business plan for the next year with goals. They all discussed the approach and what they believed would work and get them the direction they needed. They further discussed how to stay on the right path once the plan had been created.

Tom had many friends in his personal business and he focused on repairs of late model cars. His clientele was quite diverse, with some being business owners. In his discussion with one significant business owner, he was given the name and number of a business coach that could not only help create the business plan for the next year, but also provide continuous coaching thereafter to help ensure actual goal attainment.

Meanwhile, Dick and Harry, due to their business types, were constantly bombarded with marketing from significant sized consultant firms. Both had even had phone interviews with a couple of consultants. Both Dick and Harry shared their notes and realized that the consultants were basically offering turn key strategic planning services.

During the brothers' discussion, they all realized that they needed ongoing support, training, and accountability after the initial plan was created. While Dick and Harry each had a high workload and significant projects in hand, all thought that Tom starting the process was the best plan of action. They all agreed to be supportive.

Tom – Auto Repair Business

Tom wasted no time contacting the business coach and getting the process started. He started working with the coach at the beginning of the year, and after a few initial meetings, set out on the strategic business plan right away.

After a day of working together in a retreat style meeting, and then another week of finishing up the details, Tom had a strategic plan. Tom's excitement and sense of accomplishment hadn't been this high since he bought the business. Through the business planning process, Tom was able to learn many things about himself, about his business, and some far simpler ways to get routine tasks accomplished.

(Two years later) Tom was walking out of the closing meeting of more than doubling the size of his current location. Never before the last 24 months had his business been more profitable, as well as yielding a higher level of customer service. Tom's level of motivation and satisfaction with his business had never been higher. As he got in his car to drive home, he immediately called his business coach. Once the coach answered, he yelled into the phone, "We did it! This day would have never happened without your help!"

Dick – Construction Business

6 months after Tom had started working with the business coach, Dick had wrapped up a large project that he had underway and he thought "now is the time." Wasting not another minute, he got the name and number of Tom's business coach. Having stayed abreast of Tom's progress and path forward, Dick had a pretty good idea of how this was going to work.

Dick's biggest question was, "What does a business coach for my brother's much smaller car repair business know about the construction industry?"

In Dick's first meeting with the business coach, he poised just that question. The business coach went on to explain that all businesses are virtually the same; the same basic principles apply to all businesses. For example, strategic business planning is the same process for all businesses. Meanwhile, the business coach happened to have extensive experience with construction companies to boot!

As in the case with Tom, the business coach and Dick immediately set about creating a business plan for Dick's construction company. A very serious problem at Dick's company was the constant churn of RFP's for construction projects, estimates, negotiating contracts, getting the work done, and then chasing payments. It was a tiring, all consuming cycle.

During the first few months, Dick and the coach completed the plan and also worked on streamlining the duties of the management team and eliminated the ever present feeling of overwhelm. Gradually, change started to take hold.

6 months later, Dick's company was running smoother and the entire management team reported having significantly less stress. Also, company revenue and profits were slowly starting to climb.

18 months later, Dick had more ongoing projects than ever before with a smoother functioning company, and a better performance compared to quote on the projects. Also, customer complaints were declining. This all resulted in the bonding level for Dick's company being consistently and substantially increased. Looking back, Dick's profitability had doubled, while his top line revenue had grown by over 50%! Dick's satisfaction had never been greater.

Harry – Manufacturing Business

Harry had many irons in the fire and had impatiently waited and watched along the sidelines as Tom and Dick substantially improved their success and happiness with their businesses. Harry could not wait to get started.

12 months after Tom had gotten started with the business coach, Harry realized he needed to stop making excuses. Harry's biggest apprehension in working with the business coach was the time element. His second biggest apprehension was again; what does this guy know about manufacturing? Harry had also sporadically been using the services of a governmental agency that specialized in helping manufacturing companies. Harry frequently lamented that their assistance was often very theoretical and not often grounded in what really worked in the "real world."

During Harry's initial interview with the business coach, he really focused on "what do you know about manufacturing?" And, "how practical is your approach to helping my business?" Even though Harry had witnessed the huge successes that Tom and Dick were having, he was still very skeptical. However, during the interview process, the business coach allayed all of Harry's concerns and he became highly motivated to move forward.

Harry began the engagement with a high level of energy and motivation. He was thrilled to finally have a plan that he could believe in to move the business forward. During the process, Harry became critically aware that his plan, while doable, was very ambitious and he was going to need to involve his team to ever have a hope of accomplishing it.

Harry had approximately 200 employees at his manufacturing plant, with 25 salaried staff members other than himself. Of the 25, 18 employees were foremen, supervisors and managers. Harry knew he was going to need their help in order to ever have a hope of accomplishing his plan. Harry was a good delegator of the day-to-day running of his plant. He also had a very capable staff that worked very hard for the modest success they were achieving. But Harry had no idea how to begin engaging his staff to help accomplish his plan

Working with his business coach, Harry laid out a plan of company meetings to communicate his plan to the whole team, and the critical details to his management staff. This was accomplished in a tactical way, designed to gain buy in, excitement, and commitment to the plan. To Harry's surprise, the plan worked almost like magic.

One of the biggest goals that Harry had was to computerize his batching process of raw materials. His theory was better raw materials in; better product out. While he knew his plan was sound, he was aware that it was way more than he could execute and he knew his staff already worked very hard. He was concerned they would be overwhelmed in even being asked to help with the plan and might even leave over being asked to do more.

At the unveiling of his plan, the whole plant was inspired and energized. Harry was speechless. Most of the comments that he received revolved around "that's great", "this is awesome," "we have needed this so badly." So on and so forth.

Instead of Harry's fear that unveiling his plan would incite overwhelm and cause people to resign, he was pleasantly surprised that the exact opposite response happened. The employees all asked what they could do to help and offered to pitch in. His management team vowed to get this accomplished even quicker than the time line Harry laid out.

Much to Harry's surprise, they all did exactly that. Harry's computerized batching process was installed under budget and quicker than estimated. Furthermore, in Harry's small industry, there was such a fervor about Harry's project and his team's performance that people of all skill levels began knocking on his door wanting to join his team. He became an employer of choice in his market.

Author's Note:

The examples of Tom, Dick and Harry have been changed to "protect the innocent!" These are actually real examples that have occurred with clients during the life of Paramount Business Development. While the examples have been offered "tongue in cheek" for your enjoyment, they represent real examples that could happen with your company.

The individual case studies are real specific examples highlighting a specific task within the whole of strategic planning. This could be you too!

If you are new to strategic business planning, forge ahead with confidence!

About the Author:

Rick Munson is a certified Business/Executive Coach, with over 30 years of experience, whose expert strategic business planning and leadership/team development skills have led organizations through turnaround situations, out of labor difficulties and strikes, and revitalized old manufacturing plants. While he was a business coach for one of the top business improvement organizations in the world, he was awarded Global Top 100 Coach many times, and achieved the level of Platinum Master Mentor Business Coach. He also earned a North American Region award for Consistency of Client Results. Today he is President and CEO at Paramount Business Development, Inc., a company that he founded over 12 years ago, and has been coaching business owners and executives to greater success along with his partner, Bill Skinner, ever since. He has 3 children and lives in the Pocono Mountains of Pennsylvania with his wife Cheryl, daughter Nicole, and their two dogs, Hook and Bell.

95335857R00064

Made in the USA
Middletown, DE
25 October 2018